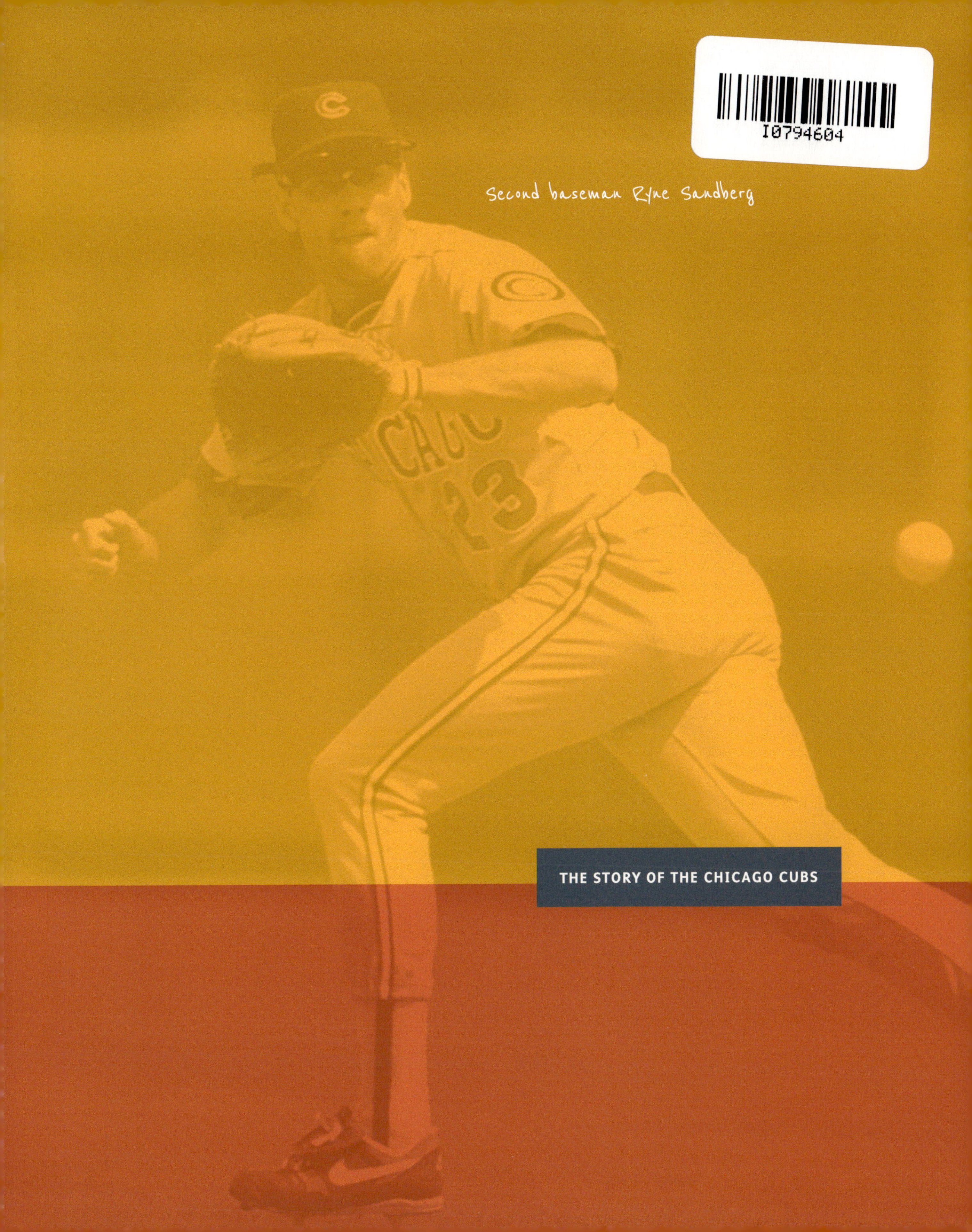

Second baseman Ryne Sandberg

THE STORY OF THE CHICAGO CUBS

Outfielder Seiya Suzuki

THE STORY OF THE

CHICAGO CUBS

JOE TISCHLER

CREATIVE SPORTS

Shortstop Ernie Banks

CREATIVE EDUCATION / CREATIVE PAPERBACKS

Published by Creative Education and Creative Paperbacks
P.O. Box 227, Mankato, Minnesota 56002
Creative Education and Creative Paperbacks are imprints of
The Creative Company
www.thecreativecompany.us

Book Design by Wyeth Morgan
Art direction by Blue Design (www.bluedes.com)

Images by Alamy Stock Photo/Nippon News, 29; Associated Press/Gareth Patterson, cover, Morry Gash, 7 (top, right); Corbis/John Zich/NewSport, 20; Getty Images/Allen Kee, 10, Bettmann, 6 (bottom, right), Chris Bernacchi/Diamond Images, 2, Chris Sweda/Chicago Tribune, 22–23, Chris Trotman, 9, Griffin Quinn, 31, Jamie Squire, 6 (top, left), John Dominis/Time Life Pictures, 7 (bottom, left), 18, Jonathan Daniel, 4–5, 32, Lee Balterman, 6 (bottom, left), Major League Baseball Photos, 10, National Baseball Hall of Fame Library, cover, 12, 15, Otto Greule Jr, 26–27, Photo File, 3, 16, Rich Pilling, 7 (bottom, right), Rob Tringali, 30, Ron Vesely, 6 (top, right), 7 (top, left), 25, Ronald C. Modra, 1, Scott Kane, 19; Shutterstock/f11photo, 11

Every effort has been made to contact copyright holders for material reproduced in this book. Any omissions will be rectified in subsequent printings if notice is given to the publisher.

Library of Congress Cataloging-in-Publication Data
Names: Tischler, Joe author
Title: The story of the Chicago Cubs / Joe Tischler.
Description: Mankato, Minnesota : Creative Education and Creative Paperbacks, 2026. | Series: Creative sports. Major League Baseball | Includes index. | Audience: Ages 8-12 | Audience: Grades 4-6 | Summary: "Discover the Chicago Cubs' thrilling journey from their early success to recent games, featuring iconic players, pivotal moments, and the Major League Baseball team's enduring resilience and determination. Written for middle-grade readers. Includes table of contents, sidebars, and index"– Provided by publisher.
Identifiers: LCCN 2025015992 (print) | LCCN 2025015993 (ebook) | ISBN 9798895810880 library binding | ISBN 9798896800415 paperback | ISBN 9798895812143 ebook
Subjects: LCSH: Chicago Cubs (Baseball team)–History–Juvenile literature
Classification: LCC GV875.C6 T57 2026 (print) | LCC GV875.C6 (ebook) | DDC 796.357/640977311–dc23/eng/20250522
LC record available at https://lccn.loc.gov/2025015992
LC ebook record available at https://lccn.loc.gov/2025015993

Printed in the United States

Pitcher Mark Prior

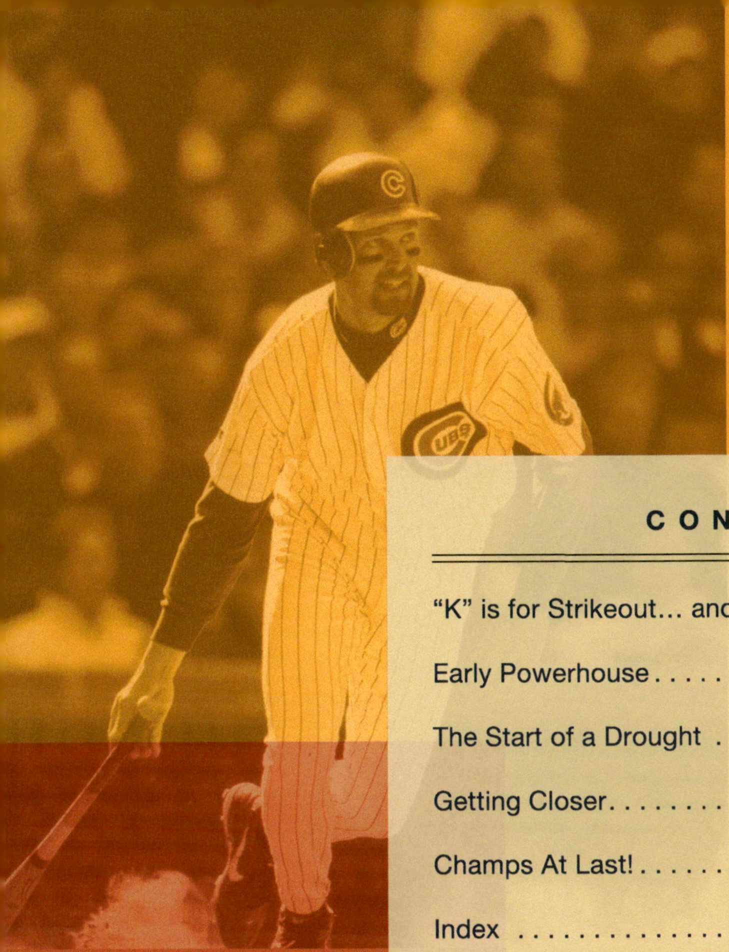
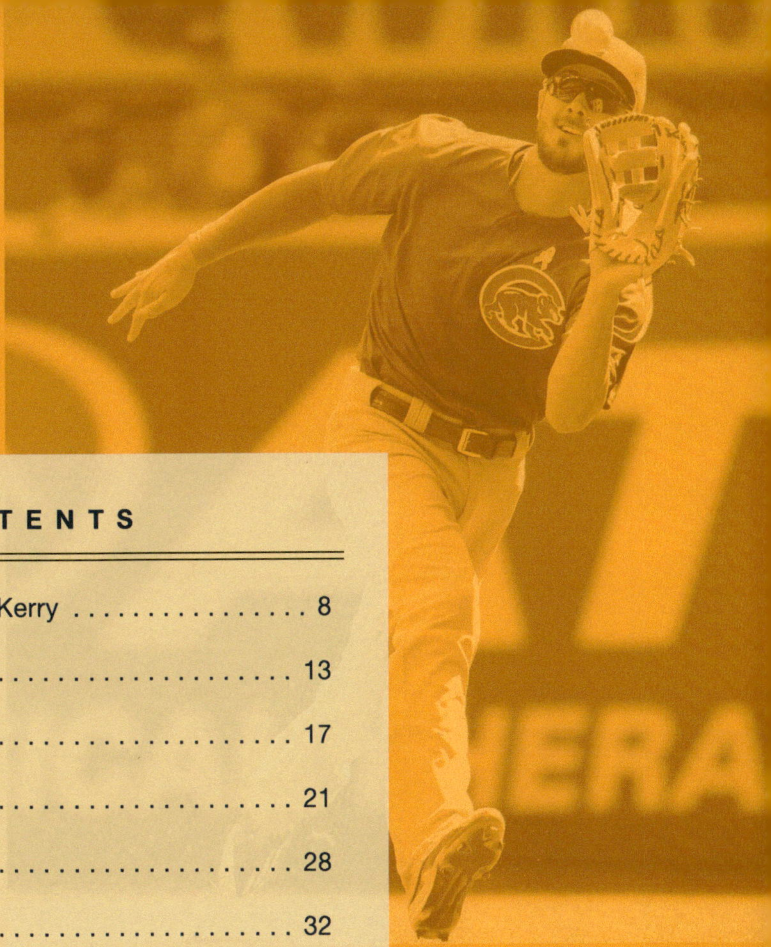

CONTENTS

EXTRA INNINGS

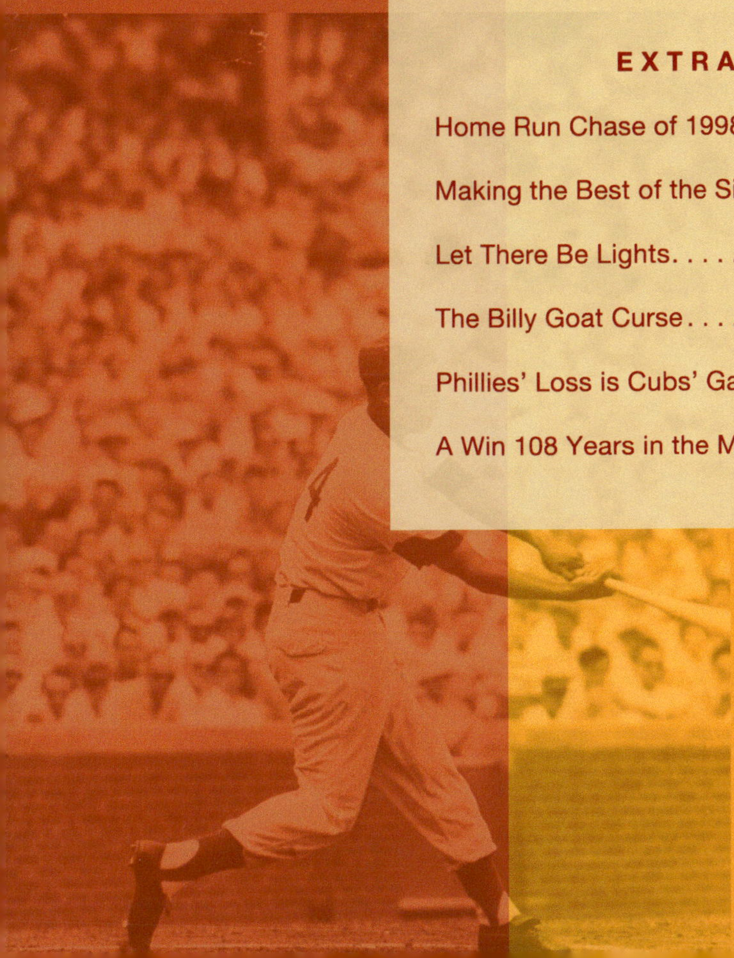

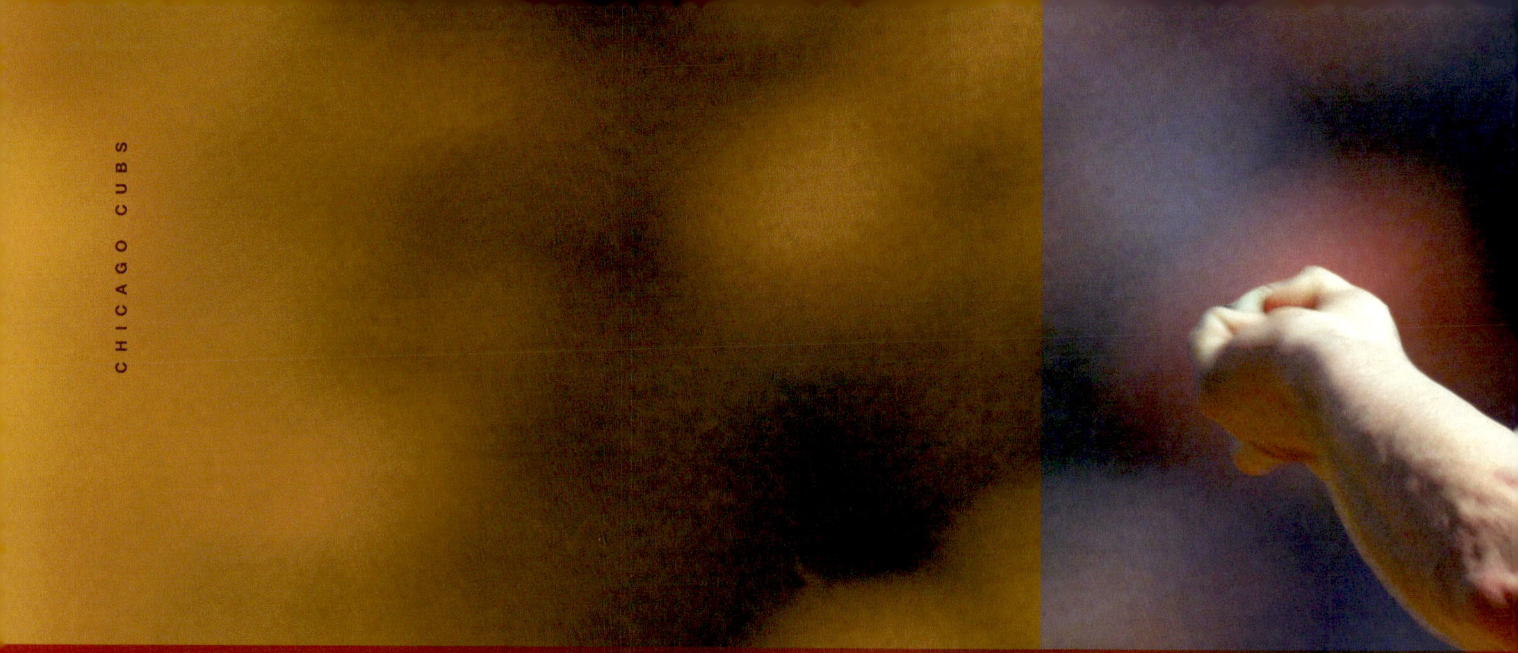

"K" IS FOR STRIKEOUT… AND KERRY

Hall of Fame pitcher Nolan Ryan holds two important Major League Baseball (MLB) records. He has the most strikeouts in MLB history with 5,714. He has also thrown the most no-hitters in MLB history with seven. The seventh and final no-hitter Ryan threw came on May 1, 1991, in Arlington, Texas. His Texas Rangers defeated the Toronto Blue Jays, 3–0. In attendance for that game was 13-year-old Kerry Wood. He grew up in nearby Irving, Texas.

Four years after that game, in 1995, Wood was drafted fourth overall by the Chicago Cubs. He worked his way through the Cubs' minor-league system over the next two and a half years. He started the 1998 season in AAA. In his lone start, he allowed just one hit and struck out 11 batters in only five innings. He was then called up to the big leagues.

Wood and the Cubs faced the Houston Astros on May 6, 1998. The game was played at Wrigley Field in Chicago, Illinois. It marked Wood's fifth MLB start. Wood wore No. 34 for the Cubs. That is the same number worn by Ryan for most of his career. On this day,

Pitcher Kerry Wood

EXTRA INNINGS

SAMMY SOSA
OUTFIELDER
CUBS SEASONS: 1992–2004
HEIGHT: 6-FOOT-0
WEIGHT: 225 POUNDS
KEY STATS: 1998 NL MVP, 7X ALL-STAR, 6X SILVER SLUGGER AWARD, 609 CAREER HOME RUNS

HOME RUN CHASE OF 1998

Prior to the 1998 season, Roger Maris held the single-season home run record. He hit 61 in 1961. St. Louis Cardinals first baseman Mark McGwire and Cubs outfielder Sammy Sosa were on a quest to beat that record in 1998. Sosa had just 13 home runs through May. He went on a tear in June. He smashed 20 long balls. That set an MLB record for most home runs in any month. McGwire still led MLB with 37 through June. McGwire was the first to reach 62 home runs on September 8. His record total reached 70. Sosa wound up with 66. He may have had the last laugh though. The Cubs made the playoffs. The Cardinals did not. Sosa was named NL Most Valuable Player (MVP).

Chicago skyline

Wood would be mentioned with Ryan with one of the greatest pitching performances of all time.

Wood was just 20 years old on that cloudy, rainy day. Houston's offense was loaded. It featured two future Hall of Famers in second baseman Craig Biggio and first baseman Jeff Bagwell. It also had six-time All-Star outfielder Moisés Alou and .300 hitter outfielder Derek Bell. The game did not start well for Wood. His first pitch of the game missed catcher Sandy Martínez's glove and hit home-plate umpire Jerry Meals in the mask. Wood settled down. He struck out Biggio, Bell, and Bagwell in the top of the first inning. Jack Howell and Alou each whiffed to start the second inning. The Cubs scored in the bottom half of the inning to take a 1–0 lead.

Ricky Gutiérrez led off the top of the third inning with a hit for Houston. The ground ball went off the glove of Cubs third baseman Kevin Orie. The play could have been called an error. It turned out to be Houston's only hit of the game.

Wood returned to striking out Astros batters. He retired five in a row on strikes over the fourth and fifth innings. Wood had 11 strikeouts after five innings. "We knew we were watching something very special after a few

CHICAGO

innings," said Cubs manager Jim Riggleman. "It was just strikeout after strikeout, making some hitters–Hall of Famers–have bad days."

As the game went on, Wood got stronger. He struck out the side in both the seventh and eighth innings. His strikeout total stood at 18 through eight innings. The major league record for a nine-inning game was 20. Roger Clemens accomplished that feat twice. If Wood struck out the side again in the ninth, he would set a new MLB record with 21 strikeouts.

Wood struck out Bill Spiers to start the ninth inning. That's 19. Biggio grounded out to shortstop on the next at-bat. The opportunity to tie the record was still at stake when Bell came to the plate. On a 1–2 count, Bell swung and missed. Strikeout number 20! "It definitely was a defining moment," said Wood. "For me, it showed me that I belonged here, it's not a fluke that I'm here, I deserve to be here. I can compete at this level."

EARLY POWERHOUSE

Major League Baseball's National League (NL) formed in 1876. The Chicago White Stockings were one of its original teams. The White Stockings were a powerhouse team. They won the first NL pennant. They won five more NL pennants over the next 10 years. Infielder Cap Anson was Chicago's first star. He played 22 years with the franchise. He led the NL in batting four times. The club changed its name to the Colts in 1890. It finished in second place the next two years. After that,

First baseman Cap Anson

the team slipped in the standings. It became the Orphans in 1898. But the name change did not help.

In 1902, management began to fill the roster with rookies and young players. A Chicago newspaper referred to the youngsters as the "Cubs." The team soon adopted it as the official name.

The team became consistent winners. The Cubs won 116 games in 1906. That remained a major-league record for nearly 100 years. The 2001 Seattle Mariners tied the mark. The Cubs accomplished their feat in fewer games than Seattle. Their .763 winning percentage remains the best in MLB history. Both teams, however, failed to win the World Series. The Cubs lost to crosstown rival Chicago White Sox in six games. The heart of that Cubs team was a famous double-play trio. It included first baseman Frank Chance, second baseman Johnny Evers, and shortstop Joe Tinker. Pitcher Mordecai Brown ruled the mound with 26 wins.

The Cubs rebounded from the World Series loss to win the NL pennant again the following season. They won 107 games. They met the Detroit Tigers in the World Series. This time, the Cubs won! They swept the series, though one game did end in a tie due to darkness. The Cubs beat the Tigers again in the World Series in 1908. This time it took five games. Little did Cubs fans know that this would mark the team's last World Series championship for over 100 years.

The Cubs returned to the World Series in 1910. But they lost to the Philadelphia Athletics in five games. The five-year stretch from 1906 to 1910 is one of the greatest in MLB history. The team averaged 106 regular-season wins and appeared in the World Series four times.

In 1916, the Cubs moved to Weeghman Park. Later, it would be called Cubs Park and then Wrigley Field. The ballpark is noted for ivy-covered outfield walls, a classic marquee sign, and an old-fashioned scoreboard.

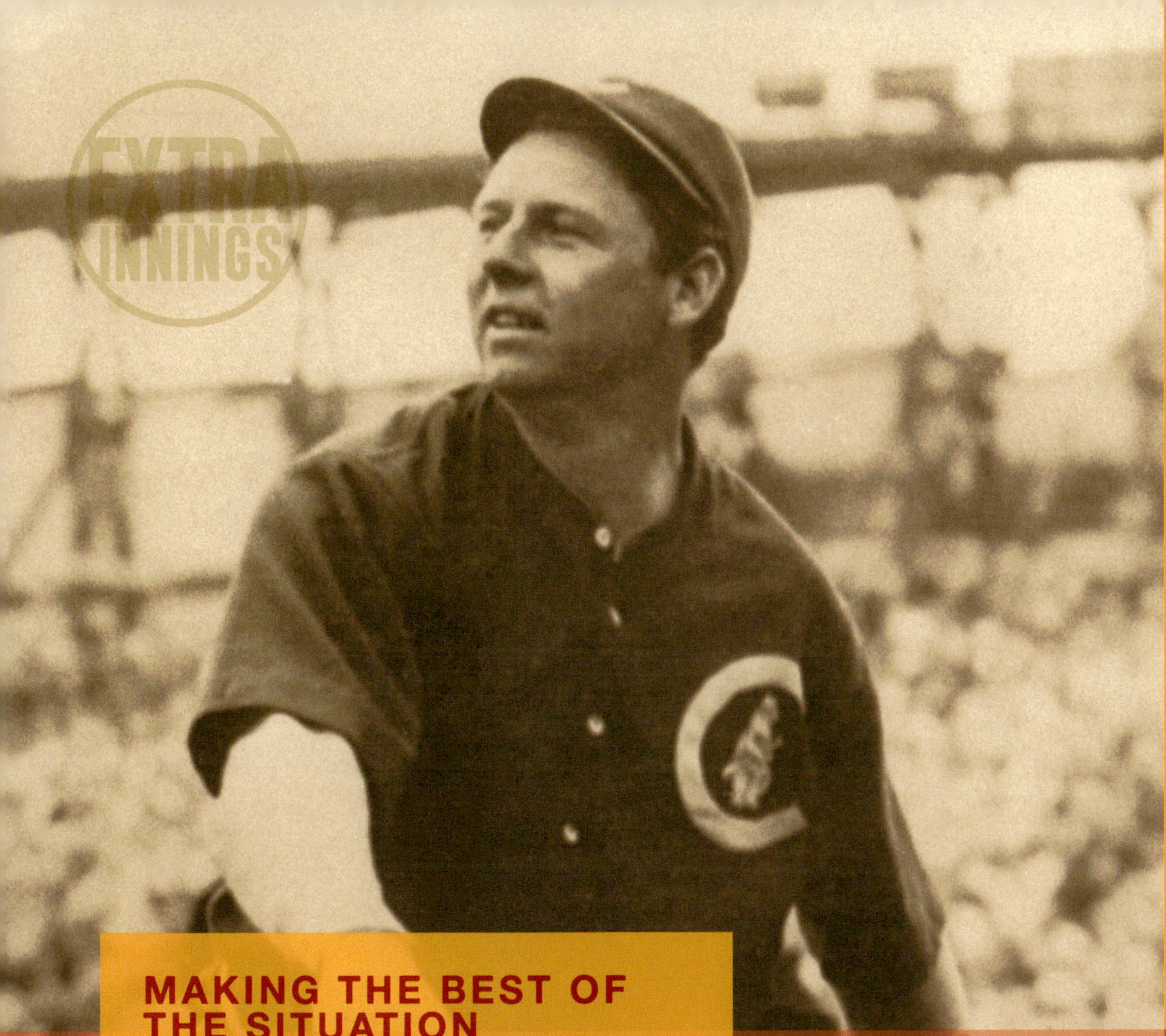

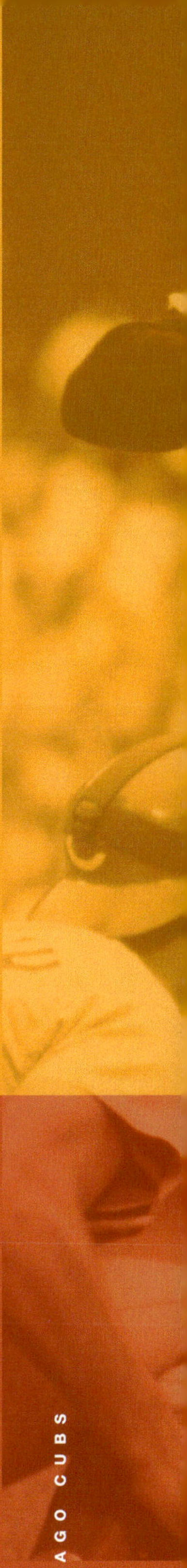

MAKING THE BEST OF THE SITUATION

As a child, Mordecai Brown suffered a farming machine accident. His right index finger was a mere stump. Not long afterward, he fell while chasing a rabbit. He broke the other fingers on his right hand. Brown was left with a crooked middle finger and a paralyzed pinky. The odd combination gave him a unique grip. His pitches had excellent movement. It was much like the split-finger fastball thrown by pitchers today. “It didn’t only curve, it curved and dropped at the same time,” a relative explained. “It made it extremely hard to hit and if you did hit it, you hit it into the ground [because you] couldn’t get under it.”

MORDECAI “THREE FINGER” BROWN
PITCHER
CUBS SEASONS: 1904–12, 1916
HEIGHT: 5-FOOT-10
WEIGHT: 175 POUNDS
KEY STATS: 1949 HALL OF FAME INDUCTEE, 2X WORLD SERIES CHAMPION, 239 CAREER WINS, 1,375 CAREER STRIKEOUTS

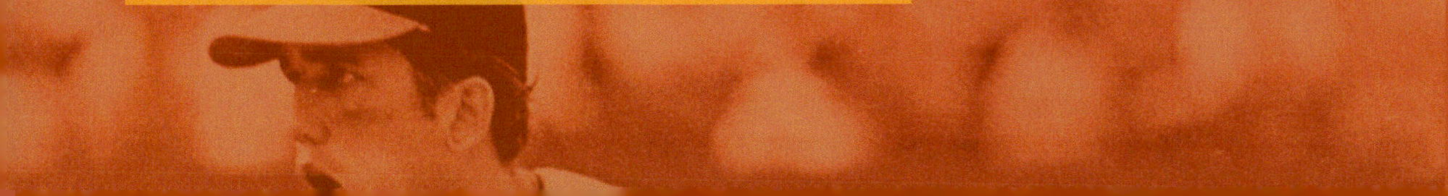

EXTRA INNINGS

LET THERE BE LIGHTS

MLB's first night game was played in 1935. Soon, nearly every team routinely played under the lights. But the Cubs refused. They became a symbol of a bygone baseball era. The franchise was sold to the Tribune Company in 1981. It wanted a more fan-friendly schedule. That meant installing lights at Wrigley Field. It would allow people to attend games after work. Neighbors objected. They did not want to deal with nighttime noise and congestion. They took the Cubs to court. The issue was finally resolved. The first official night game at Wrigley Field was played on August 9, 1988. The Cubs defeated the New York Mets, 6–4.

Ernie Banks starred for the Cubs in the 1950s and '60s. He praised the field's neighborhood atmosphere. "Wrigley is like another home in the community," he said. "When you're in Wrigley, it's like you're visiting the family of all the people that live around here."

THE START OF A DROUGHT

In 1918, the Cubs returned to the World Series. They faced the Boston Red Sox. It was a tight, low-scoring series. The Cubs scored just a total of 10 runs in six games. Boston had fewer runs with nine but won the series.

Center fielder Hack Wilson was a power-hitting force. He hit 39 home runs and drove in 159 runs in 1929. He did even better the following year. He smashed 56 home runs and set a single-season MLB record with 191 runs batted in. The Cubs won the NL pennant in 1929. It started a great 10-year stretch where the team made the World Series four times. They lost them all. The Athletics topped them in five games in 1929. The New York Yankees swept the Cubs in both the 1932 and 1938 World Series. The Cubs led MLB with 100 wins in 1935. But they lost to the Tigers in six games in the World Series.

After several losing seasons, the Cubs returned to the World Series in 1945. They fell to the Tigers again. This time, the series went the full seven games.

A long postseason drought started the following season. Chicago did not return to the playoffs for nearly 40 years. The team had plenty of stars during the lean years though. Billy Williams excelled during the 1960s and early '70s.

Shortstop Ernie Banks

He was a dangerous hitter and a dependable left fielder. Nine-time All-Star Ron Santo provided power at third base. Don Kessinger was a slick shortstop.

Perhaps the most beloved player was "Mr. Cub," Ernie Banks. He joined the team in 1953. He was the Cubs' first Black player. The shortstop won back-to-back NL Most Valuable Player (MVP) awards in 1958 and 1959. He played the last half of his career at first base following a knee injury. He retired after the 1971 season. He finished his career with 512 home runs. But he never played in a postseason game.

Pitcher Fergie Jenkins was another bright spot during the team's prolonged slump. Jenkins ranks among the best pitchers in MLB history. He won at least 20 games each year from 1967 to 1972. In each of those seasons, he threw at least 20 complete games. In his 10 years with the Cubs, Jenkins won 167 games.

MLB split into two divisions in each league in 1969. The Cubs played in the NL East Division. They led the division by nine games on August 16. The Cubs started consistently losing. The New York Mets kept winning. Chicago ended up eight games behind the Mets in the final standings.

Pitcher Drew Smyly

EXTRA INNINGS

THE BILLY GOAT CURSE

The Cubs won two of the first three games of the 1945 World Series against the Detroit Tigers. Game 4 was played at Wrigley Field. Billy Sianis owned Chicago's Billy Goat Tavern. He decided to bring the bar's mascot, an actual goat named Murphy, to the game. The goat's smell bothered other fans. Sianis and Murphy were told to leave. The Cubs lost the game. Sianis was angry. He sent a message to Cubs owner Philip K. Wrigley that read, "You are going to lose this World Series... You are never going to win a World Series again because you insulted my goat." The Cubs went on to lose the World Series. The "Curse of the Billy Goat" had begun. It struck again and again until the Cubs finally won the World Series in 2016.

Pitcher Bruce Sutter and left fielder Dave Kingman provided some highlights during the late 1970s. But by 1981, the Cubs had missed the playoffs for 35 seasons in a row.

The franchise came under new ownership that season. The Tribune Company (owner of the *Chicago Tribune* newspaper) bought it. The team added talented young players. One was outfielder and first baseman Leon Durham. Another was second baseman Ryne Sandberg.

GETTING CLOSER

In 1984, team owners invited Sianis's nephew, Sam, to opening day at Wrigley Field. Sam brought a descendent of Murphy onto the field. It seemed to help. Burly pitcher Rick Sutcliffe put up a 16–1 record. He won the NL Cy Young Award. This award is given to the league's best pitcher. The Cubs won the NL East. They finally returned to the playoffs for the first time since 1945. They won the first two games of the best-of-five NL Championship Series (NLCS) against the San Diego Padres. But the Padres won the next three. The Cubs were eliminated.

Sandberg became the face of the franchise in the 1980s. He was a model of consistency both at the plate and in the field. He led the league in fielding percentage four times. That resulted in nine career Gold Glove awards. The best fielders in each league win them. He was named NL MVP in 1984. He batted .314 and led MLB with 19 triples.

The Cubs had losing records the next four years. A bright spot was the signing of Andre "The Hawk" Dawson. He belted 49 home runs and drove in

Third baseman Kris Bryant

GALVIS
13

137 runs. Both led the NL. Despite the team finishing in last place in the NL East, Dawson was named NL MVP.

Chicago's next winning season was the team's next postseason appearance. The Cubs won the NL East in 1989. They faced the San Francisco Giants in the NLCS. First baseman Mark Grace was great in the series. He had 11 hits in five games. But the Cubs were again denied a World Series berth.

Dawson left Chicago in 1992. Young Sammy Sosa replaced him. Sosa combined the enthusiasm of Ernie Banks with the raw power of Hack Wilson. Sosa grew up in the Dominican Republic. Scouts noticed the potential of his powerful, lightning-quick bat. The Texas Rangers signed him at age 16 in 1985. By 1998, he was a star power hitter for the Cubs.

The Cubs became a point of national interest in 1998. The single-season home run pursuit of Sosa and Mark McGwire captivated the sports world. So did the strong arm of rookie pitcher Kerry Wood. The 20-strikeout game against the Houston Astros was breathtaking. Wood amassed a 13–6 record in 1998. He was named NL Rookie of the Year.

Sosa had started one of the greatest four-year stretches in MLB history in 1998. He finished with 66 home runs and an MLB-leading 158 runs batted in that season. His MVP season helped the Cubs reach the postseason. After defeating the Giants in a Wild Card tiebreaker, the Cubs were swept by the Atlanta Braves in the NL Division Series. The following year, Sosa belted 63 more home runs. He hit only 50 in 2000. But that led MLB. He was back over 60 in 2001 when he hit 64. He is the only player in MLB history to hit at least 60 home runs in three seasons.

Outfielder Andre Dawson

RYNE SANDBERG
SECOND BASEMAN
CUBS SEASONS: 1982–94, 1996–97
HEIGHT: 6-FOOT-1
WEIGHT: 175 POUNDS
KEY STATS: 2005 HALL OF FAME INDUCTEE, 1984 NL MVP, 10X ALL-STAR, 9X GOLD GLOVE

PHILLIES LOSS IS CUBS GAIN

Infielder Ryne Sandberg was drafted by the Philadelphia Phillies in the 20th round of the 1978 MLB Draft. He made his MLB debut in 1981 with the team. He only had six at-bats with one hit. The Phillies had established starters in the infield. So they traded him after the season to the Cubs. Sandberg became a regular starter at third base in 1982. The following year, he shifted to second base. That is where he earned his acclaim. He won his first of nine straight Gold Glove Awards at the position that year. He was also great with the bat. He won seven Silver Slugger Awards. The best hitters at each position win them. He was inducted into the Baseball Hall of Fame in 2005.

EXTRA INNINGS

CHAMPS AT LAST!

After two poor seasons, the Cubs began to turn things around in the new millennium. They compiled an 88–74 record in 2001. They missed the playoffs. But the season fanned the flames of hope at Wrigley Field.

Chicago posted another 88–74 season in 2003. It won the NL Central Division. The Cubs advanced to the NLCS against the Florida Marlins. They won three of the first five matchups. In Game 6, they were up 3–0 in the eighth inning. The Curse struck again. A Marlin popped a foul ball toward the left field stands. A Cubs fan interfered with the catch. Then, normally sure-handed shortstop Alex Gonzalez booted a grounder. It could have been an inning-ending double play. Instead, the Marlins went on to score eight runs. Florida won the game. They won Game 7, too. "It has nothing to do with the Curse," manager Dusty Baker said of the Game 6 loss. "It has to do with fan interference and a very uncharacteristic error."

The Cubs missed the playoffs the next three seasons. The team won the NL Central in 2007. But they were swept out of the playoffs by the Arizona Diamondbacks. Chicago did even better in 2008. It led the NL with 97 wins. They recorded their 10,000th franchise win in April. Eight players went to the All-Star Game. That set an NL record. But all their accolades did not translate to postseason success. The Los Angeles Dodgers swept them from the playoffs.

Years of struggling and rebuilding followed. Joe Maddon was hired as manager in 2015. He helped the Cubs win 97 games that year. They had won only 73 the prior year. They beat the Pittsburgh Pirates in the Wild Card game. Then they beat the Cardinals in the NL Division Series (NLDS). But they could not sustain that momentum. They fell to the New York Mets in the NLCS.

2016 WORLD SERIES
GAME 7
CHICAGO CUBS AT
CLEVELAND INDIANS
NOVEMBER 2, 2016

EXTRA INNINGS

A WIN 108 YEARS IN THE MAKING

Cubs fans had been waiting since 1908 to win a World Series. On this night, they were a few innings from capturing that elusive title. The Cubs led Cleveland 6–3 after six innings. The Indians tied the game in the eighth inning. Both teams were scoreless in the ninth. It was on to extra innings. Before the 10th inning began, a light rain began to fall. The umpires suspended play. Both teams went to their clubhouses. Cubs right fielder Jason Heyward gathered his teammates. “We’re the best team in baseball, and we’re the best team in baseball for a reason,” he said. “Now we’re going to show it. We play like the score is nothing–nothing ... Stick together and we’re going to win this game.” And win they did. The Cubs scored twice in the top of the 10th. They won 8–7. The Cubs were World Series champions.

Pitcher Shota Imanaga

Hopes were high in 2016. The Cubs did not disappoint. They won 103 games. That led all of MLB. Third baseman Kris Bryant capped a remarkable four-year run. He became the first player to win College Player of the Year, Minor League Player of the Year, Rookie of the Year, and MVP in successive years. Chicago brushed aside the Giants in the NLDS. They topped the Dodgers in six games to win their first NL pennant since 1945. Then, after falling behind three games to one against the Cleveland Indians in the World Series, the Cubs clawed their way back to win their first World Series title in 108 years.

The Cubs returned to the playoffs the next two years. The Dodgers got their revenge in the 2017 NLCS, and the Cubs lost to the Rockies in the 2018 Wild Card game. The Cubs won the NL Central in a COVID-shortened 2020 season, going 34–26 before falling to the Marlins in the Wild Card round. Two losing seasons followed. Chicago finished 83–79 in both 2023 and 2024 but missed the postseason. In 2025, the Cubs finally returned to October baseball. They went 92–70, finished second in the NL Central, and earned a Wild Card berth. They beat the Padres before dropping a five-game NLDS to the Brewers.

Few teams in any professional sport can boast the rich history and tradition of the Chicago Cubs. Fewer still can claim the fierce fan loyalty the team has enjoyed through good times and bad. As the wind from Lake Michigan blows into Chicago each spring, it brings the possibility that once again, the Cubs will win it all.

Outfielder Ian Happ

INDEX